ASTROLOGY
SELF-CARE

Virgo

ASTROLOGY SELF-CARE

Virgo

Live your best life by the stars

Sarah Bartlett

First published in Great Britain in 2022 by Yellow Kite
An imprint of Hodder & Stoughton
An Hachette UK company

1

Copyright © Sarah Bartlett 2022

The right of Sarah Bartlett to be identified as the Author
of the Work has been asserted by her in accordance
with the Copyright, Designs and Patents Act 1988.

Illustrations © shutterstock.com

A CIP catalogue record for this title is
available from the British Library

Hardback ISBN 978 1 399 70473 1
eBook ISBN 978 1 399 70474 8
Audiobook ISBN 978 1 399 70475 5

Designed by Goldust Design

Typeset in Nocturne Serif by Hewer Text UK Ltd, Edinburgh
Printed and bound in Great Britain by Clays Ltd, Elcograf S.p.A.

Hodder & Stoughton policy is to use papers that are
natural, renewable and recyclable products and made
from wood grown in sustainable forests. The logging and
manufacturing processes are expected to conform to the
environmental regulations of the country of origin.

Yellow Kite
Hodder & Stoughton Ltd
Carmelite House
50 Victoria Embankment
London EC4Y 0DZ

www.yellowkitebooks.co.uk

Delicious autumn! My very soul is wedded to it,
and if I were a bird I would fly about the earth
seeking the successive autumns.

George Eliot, English novelist

There is a path, hidden between the road of reason and the hedgerow of dreams, which leads to the secret garden of self-knowledge. This book will show you the way.

Contents

Introduction

The ancient Greek goddess Gaia arose from Chaos and was the personification of the Earth and all of Nature. One of the first primordial beings, along with Tartarus (the Underworld), Eros (love) and Nyx (night), as mother of all life, she is both the embodiment of all that this planet is and its spiritual caretaker.

It's hardly likely you will want to become a full-time Mother Earth, but many of us right now are caring more about our beautiful planet and all that lives upon it. To nurture and respect this amazing place we call home, and to preserve this tiny dot in the Universe, the best place to start is, well, with you.

Self-care is about respecting and honouring who you are as an individual. It's about realising that nurturing yourself is neither vanity nor a conceit, but a creative act that brings an awesome sense of awareness and a deeper connection to the Universe and all that's in it. Caring about yourself means you care about everything in the cosmos – because you are part of it.

But self-care isn't just about trekking to the gym, jogging around the park or eating the right foods. It's also about discovering who you are becoming as an individual and caring for that authenticity (and loving and caring about who we are becoming means others can love and care about us, too). This is where the art of sun-sign astrology comes in.

Astrology and Self-Care

So what is astrology? And how can it direct each of us to the right self-care pathway? Put simply, astrology is the study of the planets, sun and moon and their influence on events and people here on Earth. It is an art that has been used for thousands of years to forecast world events, military and political outcomes and, more recently, financial market trends. As such, it is an invaluable tool for understanding our own individuality and how to be true to ourselves. Although there is still dispute within astrological circles as to whether the planets actually physically affect us, there is strong evidence to show that the cycles and patterns they create in the sky have a direct mirroring effect on what happens down here on Earth and, more importantly, on each individual's personality.

Your horoscope or birth-chart is a snapshot of the planets, sun and moon in the sky at the moment you were born. This amazing picture reveals all your innate potential, characteristics and qualities. In fact, it is probably the best 'selfie' you could ever have! Astrology can not only tell you who you are, but also how best to care for that self and your own specific needs and desires as revealed by your birth-chart.

Self-care is simply time to look after yourself – to restore, inspirit and refresh and love your unique self.

But it's also about understanding, accepting and being aware of your own traits – both the good and not so good – so that you can then say, 'It's ok to be me, and my intention is to become the best of myself'. In fact, by looking up to the stars and seeing how they reflect us down here on Earth, we can deepen our connection to the Universe for the good of all, too. Understanding that caring about ourselves is not selfish creates an awesome sense of self-acceptance and awareness.

So how does each of us honour the individual 'me' and find the right kind of rituals and practices to suit our personalities? Astrology sorts us out into the zodiac – an imaginary belt encircling the Earth divided into twelve sun signs; so, for example, what one sign finds relaxing, another may find a hassle or stressful. When it comes to physical fitness, adventurous Arians thrive on aerobic work, while soulful Pisceans feel nurtured by yoga. Financial reward or status would inspire the ambitious Capricorn mind, while theatrical Leos need to indulge their joy of being centre stage.

By knowing which sun sign you are and its associated characteristics, you will discover the right self-care routines and practices to suit you. And this unique and empowering book is here to help – with all the rituals and practices in these pages specifically suited to your sun-sign personality for nurturing and vitalising your mind, body and spirit.

However, self-care is not an excuse to be lazy and avoid the goings on in the rest of the world. Self-care is about taking responsibility for our choices and understanding our unique essence, so that we can engage with all aspects of ourselves and the way we interact with the world.

IN A NUTSHELL

The sophisticated, kind-hearted, hard-working Virgo belies a sensitive soul, often sacrificed in their need to be of service to others. Like the other Earth signs, Virgos are producers and they like to be the ones making the plans. Always enthusiastic about helping others feel good about themselves, Virgos busy themselves by researching the latest remedies and health-care products, making sure that all the knowledge they acquire can be put to constructive and positive use. But to restore, nourish and vitalise Virgos' potential for being the most self-contained and yet sympathetic of signs, they need to learn to care for themselves first, and others second. This will boost their self-esteem, enhance their skills, nurture their sacred selves and bring their souls alive.

Sun-Sign Astrology

Also known as your star sign or zodiac sign, your sun sign encompasses the following:

* Your solar identity, or sense of self
* What really matters to you
* Your future intentions
* Your sense of purpose
* Various qualities that manifest through your actions, goals, desires and the personal sense of being 'you'
* Your sense of being 'centred' – whether 'self-centred' (too much ego) or 'self-conscious' (too little ego); in other words, how you perceive who you are as an individual

In fact, the sun tells you how you can 'shine' best to become who you really are.

ASTROLOGY FACTS

The zodiac or sun signs are twelve 30-degree segments that create an imaginary belt around the Earth. The zodiac belt is also known as the ecliptic, which is the apparent path of the sun as it travels round the Earth during the year.

The sun or zodiac signs are further divided into four elements (Fire, Earth, Air and Water, denoting a certain energy ruling each sign), plus three modalities (qualities associated with how we interact with the world; these are known as Cardinal, Fixed and Mutable). So as a Virgo, for example, you are a 'Mutable Earth' sign.

* Fire signs: Aries, Leo, Sagittarius
  They are: extrovert, passionate, assertive

* Earth signs: Taurus, Virgo, Capricorn
  They are: practical, materialistic, sensual

* Air signs: Gemini, Libra, Aquarius
  They are: communicative, innovative, inquisitive

* Water signs: Cancer, Scorpio, Pisces
  They are: emotional, intuitive, understanding

The modalities are based on their seasonal resonance according to the northern hemisphere.

Cardinal signs instigate and initiate ideas and projects.
They are: Aries, Cancer, Libra and Capricorn

Fixed signs resolutely build and shape ideas.
They are: Taurus, Leo, Scorpio and Aquarius

Mutable signs generate creative change and adapt ideas to reach a conclusion.
They are: Gemini, Virgo, Sagittarius and Pisces

Planetary rulers

Each zodiac sign is assigned a planet, which highlights the qualities of that sign:

Aries is ruled by Mars (fearless)
Taurus is ruled by Venus (indulgent)
Gemini is ruled by Mercury (magical)
Cancer is ruled by the moon (instinctive)
Leo is ruled by the sun (empowering)
Virgo is ruled by Mercury (informative)
Libra is ruled by Venus (compassionate)
Scorpio is ruled by Pluto (passionate)
Sagittarius is ruled by Jupiter (adventurous)
Capricorn is ruled by Saturn (disciplined)
Aquarius is ruled by Uranus (innovative)
Pisces is ruled by Neptune (imaginative)

Opposite Signs

Signs oppose one another across the zodiac (i.e. those that are 180 degrees away from each other) – for example, Virgo opposes Pisces and Aries opposes Libra. We often find ourselves mysteriously attracted to our opposite signs in romantic relationships, and while the signs' traits appear to clash in this 'polarity', the essence of each is contained in the other (note, they have the same modality). Gaining insight into the characteristics of your opposite sign (which are, essentially, inherent in you) can deepen your understanding of the energetic interplay of the horoscope.

On The Cusp

Some of us are born 'on the cusp' of two signs – in other words, the day or time when the sun moved from one zodiac sign to another. If you were born at the end or beginning of the dates usually given in horoscope pages (the sun's move through one sign usually lasts approximately four weeks), you can check which sign you are by contacting a reputable astrologer (or astrology site) (see Resources, p. 113) who will calculate it exactly for you. For example, 23 August is the standardised changeover day for the sun to move into Virgo and out of Leo. But every year, the time and even sometimes the day the sun changes sign can differ. So, say you were born on 23 August at five in the morning and the sun didn't move into Virgo until five in the afternoon on that day, you would be a Leo, not a Virgo.

How To Use This Book

The book is divided into three parts, each guiding you in applying self-care to different areas of your life:

* Part One: your mind and feelings
* Part Two: your body
* Part Three: your soul

Caring about the mind using rituals or ideas tailored to your sign shows you ways to unlock stress, restore focus or widen your perception. Applying the practices in Part One will connect you to your feelings and help you to acknowledge and become aware of why your emotions are as they are and how to deal with them. This sort of emotional self-care will set you up to deal with your relationships better, enhance all forms of communication and ensure you know exactly how to ask for what you want or need, and be true to your deepest desires.

A WORD ON CHAKRAS

Eastern spiritual traditions maintain that universal energy, known as 'prana' in India and 'chi' in Chinese philosophy, flows through the body, linked by seven subtle energy centres known as chakras (Sanskrit for 'wheel'). These energies are believed to revolve or spiral around and through our bodies, vibrating at different frequencies (corresponding to seven colours of the light spectrum) in an upward, vertical direction. Specific crystals are placed on the chakras to heal, harmonise, stimulate or subdue the chakras if imbalance is found.

The seven chakras are:
* The base or root (found at the base of the spine)
* The sacral (mid-belly)
* The solar plexus (between belly and chest)
* The heart (centre of chest)
* The throat (throat)
* The third eye (between the eyebrows)
* The crown (top of the head)

On p. 92 we will look in more detail at how Virgos can work with chakras for self-care.

Fitness and caring for the body are different for all of us, too. While Virgo benefits from a few circuits in the gym, Sagittarius prefers to trek through the mountains, and Gemini a daily quick stretch or yoga. Delve into Part Two whenever you're in need of physical restoration or a sensual makeover tailored to your sign.

Spiritual self-care opens you to your sacred self or soul. Which is why Part Three looks at how you can nurture your soul according to your astrological sun sign. It shows you how to connect to and care for your spirituality in simple ways, such as being at one with Nature or just enjoying the world around you. It will show you how to be more positive about who you are and honour your connection to the Universe. In fact, all the rituals and practices in this section will bring you joyful relating, harmonious living and a true sense of happiness.

The Key

Remember, your birth-chart or horoscope is like the key to a treasure chest containing the most precious jewels that make you you. Learn about them, and care for them well. Use this book to polish, nurture, respect and give value to the beautiful gemstones of who you are, and, in doing so, bring your potential to life. It's your right to be true to who you are, just by virtue of being born on this planet, and therefore being a child of Mother Earth and the cosmos.

Care for you, and you care for the Universe.

VIRGO
WORDS OF WISDOM

As you embark on your self-care journey, it's important to look at the lunar cycles and specific astrological moments throughout the year. At those times (and, indeed, at any time you choose), the words of Virgo wisdom below will be invaluable, empowering you with positive energy. Taking a few mindful moments at each of the four major phases of every lunar cycle and at the two important astrological moments in your solar year (see Glossary, p. 115) will affirm and enhance your positive attitude towards caring about yourself and the world.

NEW CRESCENT MOON – to care for yourself:

'I need to be of service to others but remember to be of service to myself.'

'I must learn to express my inner passions and desires.'

'Feeling self-contained will liberate me from the fear of being possessed by others.'

FULL MOON – for sealing your intention to care for your feeling world:

'My feelings flow through me; I accept them for being there.'

'I will be more open about expressing my love for others.'

'Being true to my instincts means I help not only others, but also myself.'

WANING MOON – for letting go, and letting things be:

'It's ok for me to have a discriminating eye, but not to overly criticise.'

'I must learn not to confuse service with sacrifice.'

'Being a Virgo is not just about seeing life as black or white; it is about seeing the myriad shades of grey.'

DARK OF THE MOON – to acknowledge your 'shadow' side:

'If things aren't in order, that doesn't mean they are wrong.'

'I will nurture myself with the support of others, rather than erect fences against their advice.'

'I will show enthusiasm and genuine admiration, not fear or coldness.'

SOLAR RETURN SALUTATION – welcoming your new solar year to be true to who you are:

Repeat on your birthday: 'I will establish exactly the kind of work–life balance that I wish to live by and honour my love of caring for the world by taking time to care for myself.'

SUN IN OPPOSITION – learn to be open to the opposite perspective that lies within you:

Repeat when the sun is in Pisces: 'My opposite sign is Pisces, a sign of imagination and of spiritual understanding. These attributes are in my birth-chart, too. I affirm that a sense of oneness with all those who share this planet Earth exists deep within me and I will remember to connect to this sacred place.'

The Virgo Personality

𝈨

'To dwellers in a wood, almost every species of tree has its voice as well as its feature.'
Thomas Hardy, English author and poet

Characteristics: Discriminating, selective, altruistic, incisive, hard-working, honest, practical, dedicated, self-doubting, organised, body-conscious, worrier, critical, efficient, cool, sensual, self-contained, wise, monogamous, intellectual, self-righteous, poised

Symbol: the Virgin
The second-largest constellation in the sky, Virgo (Latin for virgin) has traditionally been associated with harvest time. The ancient Babylonians knew her as the goddess of corn, Shala, while the Greeks knew her as the Earth goddess, Demeter; she was also associated with the underworld goddess, Persephone, Demeter's daughter. Since classical times, Virgo's symbol has been depicted as a maiden

carrying a sheaf of corn (the constellation's largest star, Spica, means 'ear of corn') and in medieval Europe was associated with the Virgin Mary.

Planetary ruler: Mercury

The closest planet to the sun, Mercury is also the smallest in our solar system, taking only eighty-eight days to orbit the sun. Rocky, solid and riddled with craters, like the moon, Mercury spins very slowly, and takes fifty-nine Earth days to complete one full rotation. If you were born on Mercury, you'd have a birthday every three months, but you'd only see the sun rise once every 108 days. As mercurial as you can get!

Astrological Mercury: The god Mercury (and his Greek counterpart, Hermes) was known as the messenger of the gods. He could move freely between heaven, Earth and the underworld. Mercury's attributes were associated with boundaries, travel, trade, bridges, crossroads and magic. In the birth-chart, Mercury describes the way we communicate, travel, trade, adapt to circumstances and how we relate to the world around us.

Element: Earth

Like the other Earth signs, Taurus and Capricorn, Virgo is grounded in reality and skilled at managing and using resources. Earth signs are sensual, dependable and need to be engaged with, or have some form of control of, the material world.

Modality: Mutable
Flexible, creative, spontaneous, quick-thinking, changeable, restless. As with the other Mutable signs, Gemini, Sagittarius and Pisces, Virgo marks the changeover from one season to another, in this case from summer to autumn.

Body: Diaphragm, intestines, bowels, solar plexus

Crystal: Peridot

Sun-sign profile: Virgo marks the end of summer and the start of autumn (in the northern hemisphere), a time of harvest, the falling of leaves, the altering light and Nature's seasonal change to ensure regrowth for the following year. As children of the autumn, Virgos instinctively know they must work their own 'ground', too, and harvest the results of all they have learned or processed. In this way, they acquire knowledge in spades, as long as it is useful to them. Afer all, what's the point of dreaming if one can't manifest the dream? This pragmatic approach to life means Virgo finds meaning in synthesising, classifying and ordering the world around them to get the job done – and whatever they do, they are sure to do it well.

This discriminating Earth sign also compartmentalises or sorts – anything from ideas to their sock and undies drawer. This neat orderliness is not about perfection, per se (the ideal of Libra); it's about having some kind of control over the outside world, simply because the emotional undercurrents of their inner world are *so* chaotic. In business, too, they have a natural talent for ironing out other people's mistakes with flair and sophistication, another way to maintain a tidy filing-cabinet mind. Secretive about their innermost desires and feelings (simply because their emotions are impossible to classify), Virgos are, however, the most interesting, witty, kind and sensitive of souls.

Being of service in some way is important to Virgos, and they often become the local 'carer' – the one who notices the sad child or the needy aged person in their local community. Virgos may not be able to sort out their own emotional stuff but will always lend a helping hand, and can change others' lives for the better with their wisdom and hands-on knowledge. But never forget, this pragmatic approach to life belies an earthy mysticism, and a sense of the deeper workings of the magic within themselves.

Your best-kept secret: Deep within is a hidden mystic who secretly longs to discover a connection to the divine.

What gives you meaning and purpose? The Virgo drive and purpose is to feel complete and self-contained and be of service to others.

What makes you feel good to be you? White linen, a spotless bathroom, intelligent conversation, being pampered, honesty, Nature walks, gardening, exercise, reading in bed with your partner, order in the kitchen, short trips

What or who do you identify with? Fitness professionals, editors, librarians, intellectuals, writers, workaholics, alternative health advisors, yoga gurus, dieticians, aerobic instructors

What stresses you out? Emotional scenes, ignorance, disorder, dirty fingernails, chaos, lazy people, fast-food chains, bad service, untidiness, not being in control

What relaxes you? Chatting to friends, compiling lists, researching, cupboards full of vitamins and herbs, brainy folk, puzzles, crosswords and board games, bargain hunting, gossip

What challenges you? Although you know the tangible world can be ordered and classified, trying to sort out people and pigeonhole their feelings – most of all, your own – is one of the greatest challenges for your discriminating mind.

What Does Self-Care Mean For Virgo?

With knowledge being a big part of Virgo's raison d'etre, you're probably already a bit of a self-care expert. With a mind like an encyclopaedia, you collect notes on skin products, nutrients and herbal medicine, so you are prepared to sort out everyone else's needs. You may worry about every spot on your face or negative thought in your head, and then worry about all the worrying you do. But do you really give yourself enough 'me-time' to look after yourself? Whether or not you're already an authority on healthy living, muscles, carbs and a clean environment, dive into this book right now and learn to care for you first, and everyone else second.

When Virgos put their minds to doing something – whether fixing the hole in the wall or writing a shopping list – they do it well and usually impeccably. It's all about creating something workable and, of course, useful and sellable from what they know and what they do. So by combining your talent for knowledge, earthy realism and a desire to be of service in some way, you can cultivate not only other people's self-care gardens, but your own, too. That's called self-understanding.

Self-Care Focus

You probably already know how to keep yourself in shape and look after your physical health. But why not put a few more pieces of the care puzzle on the table, and nurture your feelings, your thoughts, your loving nature and your soul, too? This book suggests new ways to fulfil your potential to feel a sense of self-containment and wholeness. You don't have to be a Mother Teresa (who was, in fact, a Virgo who synthesised mystical devotion and serving others), nor even aspire to that status, but you can aim to be a healing force for yourself and, therefore, for others. Take care of your own needs and your own emotional mystery by embracing and loving them to truly become who you are.

PART ONE

Caring For Your Mind And Feelings

The truth is obtained like gold, not by letting it grow bigger, but by washing off from it everything that isn't gold.

Leo Tolstoy, Russian writer

This section will inspire you to delight in your thoughts, express your ideas and take pleasure in your feelings. Once you get that deep sense of awareness of who you are and what you need, not only will it feel good to be alive, but you will be even more content to be yourself. The rituals and practices here will boost your self-esteem, motivate you to lead a more serene existence and enhance all forms of relationships with others. The most important relationship of all, with yourself, will be nurtured in the best possible way according to your sun sign.

It's hard to be more knowledgeable than a Virgo. You may well have a library full of books about botany, poisonous plants, bones, biology, homeopathy and Bach flower remedies – and if not, then you probably will soon. Yet, the mind isn't just a cerebral exercise in fact-finding, nor is it just a 'filing cabinet' filled with wonderful ideas; it's also about the synthesis (the Virgo 'catch word') of feeling, thought, desire and action. This section will inspire you to become aware of these processes and, in doing so, to begin to know yourself well enough to edit out the bits that are of little use, while accepting that behind that cool, pragmatic attitude lies a soulful and sensitive inner you.

The following practices will help you to see more clearly the workings of your mind – how to advance your ideas and develop a greater awareness of what knowledge means to you. They will also inspire you to let down your guard and open up to the more spontaneous and dreamy side of you. With acceptance and self-understanding, this will help you to help others better, too.

....

ENHANCE YOUR MERCURIAL MIND

✳

Colleges, libraries, bookshops and internet sites are full of dedicated, discriminating, earthy Virgos, feeding on or imparting knowledge, which is then channelled into practical, workable results. But the mind isn't just about logic and classification. It's also about imagination.

The 'caduceus' (a word rooted in the ancient Greek for 'messenger' or 'herald') was a serpent-entwined staff belonging to the god Hermes (Mercury) and symbolic of negotiation, commerce and trade; but it was also believed to have magical powers both to induce sleep and wake people from it. Use it here in this fun ritual to balance your rational mind with a more creative, intuitive process and help awaken your imagination.

You will need:
* A red tea light
* An image of the caduceus on a piece of A4 paper
* Gold glitter
* Red rose petals (dried, fresh or fake)
* A small pouch

1. On a full-moon evening, light the candle.

2. Place the image at the top of your paper, sprinkle some gold glitter across the wand, then some rose petals, and say, 'With this votive, I seal my desire to awaken my imagination, and enhance all creative ideas'.

3. Focus on the image of the wand for a minute or two, then remove the candle and blow it out, well away from the glitter (or the gold will go everywhere!).

4. Leave the symbolic offering overnight, and the next morning, fold the paper carefully around the rose petals and glitter and place in the pouch.

Keep the pouch in a safe place and repeat the ritual whenever you want to regenerate or enhance your Virgo imagination.

A GARDEN OF KNOWLEDGE

♡

Astrologically, the symbol of the maiden carrying the sheaf is associated with both Persephone, goddess of the underworld and spring, and also her mother Demeter, the goddess of the Earth, harvest and fertility. This mythic connection means Virgo has a profound yet unconscious understanding of the cycles and dynamics of the natural world, and often gets bothered by ecological, environmental or planetary issues. Try to harness this underlying niggle by creating a journal in which you can collate and organise all this information and make sense of it.

1. Find a beautiful journal, writing book, sketch book – anything that makes you go, 'Ah, that's special for me'.

2. Collect images, ideas, quotes and affirmations, news items that appeal to you (maybe to do with climate change, global warming, food chains, plastics, sustainable sources) and which you can assemble in your book, as if it were a kitchen garden filled with useful ingredients.

3. As you collect, open your mind to a bigger perspective – maybe include images or symbolic associations with issues such as planetary wobble, the state of the solar system, outer space, black holes and so on.

Turn to this journal as your garden of knowledge, ever growing, seeding new ideas, ready to be harvested when needed. It will help you to classify, organise and find clarity in resolving any niggles in the back of your mind.

....

SELL YOUR IDEAS

Ruled by Mercury, the god of trade and commerce, Virgos like to use information in a profitable way. With the help of this ritual, you can market your plans and be so persuasive you could sell cacti in the desert. This will promote your sense of achievement, too.

You will need:
* Paints or permanent markers
* 4 smooth stones or pebbles (or scraps of paper)
* 4 white tea lights
* A small box or pouch

1. Paint or draw the symbol for your ruler, Mercury, on each of the four pebbles or scraps of paper.

2. Mark each pebble or paper with the following letters to represent the elements: on the first an 'E' for earth; on the second an 'A' for air; on the third an 'F' for fire; and on the fourth a 'W' for water.

3. Place the candles in a group on a table you can walk around (or on the floor, if that's not possible).

4. Space the pebbles or papers about 13cm (5 inches) apart, with the earth one to the west, the air one to the east, the fire one to the south and the water one to the north.

5. Walk around the table or the arrangement on the floor in an anticlockwise direction four times, then say:

All of my knowledge fuels my desire

To bring achievement to which I aspire

So others will hear me and be impressed

These ideas will sell, for this I am blessed.

6. Blow out the candles and place the stones in the box or pouch.

Keep the box or pouch in the room, study or office where you do most of your business or work. If you perform this ritual before starting any new project, you'll be able to negotiate and attract the necessary contacts to fulfil all aspects of your plan for success.

....

SELF–BELIEF VISION BOWL

✳

Being a bit of a workaholic is no bad thing and, as any Virgo knows, good results are the product of all that's stored in your brightly lit mind – all that you sift, discern and classify. Yet the pressure of work can give you the odd twinge of self-doubt and worry that you're not doing enough to make things, well, work. To solve this, create the simple vision bowl below, filled with empowering crystals.

You will need:

* A smallish, unassuming (you know you hate to be flash) bowl
* 3 peridot tumbled stones
* 3 sodalite tumbled stones
* 3 moss-agate tumbled stones
* Frankincense essential oil

1. Place all the stones in your bowl and stir them around a little with your finger, while you say: 'These stones will bring mental clarity and clear my mind of uncertainty. I will not question myself, only answer to myself.'

2. Drizzle a couple of drops of the frankincense oil into the bowl.

3. Place the bowl in a discreet place, even a drawer if you're working with others and feel shy about having a little magic charm on your desk.

4. You will soon find that you have vanquished self-doubt and are blessed with self-belief, self-confidence and an incisive mind.

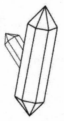

....

THE 'SOPHISTICAT' IN YOU

♡

Virgos' refined thinking, good taste and precise and intelligent forethought are encapsulated in the word sophistication (that's in its modern usage, as opposed to in medieval Europe, where it was a term of contempt). Yet it's not so easy to accept, acknowledge or express this quality when you are used to holding up a smokescreen of modest endeavour.

In ancient Egypt, the 'domestic cat' was respected, worshipped and treated as a cultural icon, and was identified with the goddess Bastet. Cats are aloof, independent, confident and worldly-wise. Draw on this cat-like confidence (as symbolised by the crystal cat's eye or tiger's eye) to boost your own inner self-esteem and to enhance that Virgo sense of poise and elegance.

You will need:
* 3 cat's eye or tiger's eye crystals
* 1 red tea light

1. On the evening of a new crescent moon, form a triangle with the three crystals on your table.

2. Light the candle and place it in the middle of your triangle.

3. Take up the crystals in turn and blow one long out-breath on each of them to imbue them with your refined energy before replacing them.

4. After you have replaced the crystals, say: 'With these crystals, I am inspirited with the power of my own grace, finesse and discernment'.

5. Blow out the candle.

Leave the arrangement overnight, and the next day you'll feel like the prized 'sophisticat' of the zodiac. Perform this practice at every new moon to help restore your urbane self-esteem.

ALL CHANGE

There are times when even the most dedicated, industrious Virgo needs to stop what they're doing – even if just for a few minutes – take a break and clear their mind. Here's a simple way to stop the clock briefly, enjoy some peace from the busy workings of your mind and recharge your mental batteries.

You will need:
* A clock, alarm or mobile-phone alarm – whichever you prefer
* A large round, oval or flat polished piece of obsidian

1. Set your clock for your chosen hour, say about two hours after you've begun your work (and at the same time every day).

2. When the alarm rings, without hesitation stop what you are doing, down tools and pick up your obsidian.

3. Walk purposefully away from your work space, and out of the room.

4. Go outside or into another room – anywhere, as long as you change your space.

5. Close your eyes and hold up the obsidian to your third-eye chakra (located between your eyebrows, just above the bridge of your nose) and say, 'I now cleanse my mind of all debris, pollution and overloaded thoughts. I am mentally revived and ready to restart.'

6. Repeat five times (so that's six in total – Virgo's associated number).

7. Return to your workplace feeling restored, rested and filled with clarity.

Getting out of the routine work zone in this way helps the Virgo mind to assimilate new ideas and process old ones. You can also do this simple exercise whenever you need to create a channel for a positive mindset.

DESTRESSING RITUAL

✳

Now, Virgos have to admit to being the first to get stressed about anything resembling disorder. That 'disorder' can also present itself when their neat mind can't find a way to assimilate the facts or make sense of things. For Virgos, 'making sense' is a way to close the metaphorical door on the world of emotions that create a sense of chaos. So to alleviate stress, and restore a feeling of making sense, try this calming incense-burning ritual.

You will need:
* A white tea light
* Sandalwood incense

1. Find a quiet place, just for once, and chill.

2. Light your candle and incense, and gaze at the candle flame.

3. As the incense begins to fill the room, imagine you are burning all the bad 'senselessness' out of your mind and body. The stresses of your body are being smoked out and released into the atmosphere, while the candle flame and the incense purge you of all those negative impulses.

4. Sit quietly for about five minutes or so, then blow out the candle.

Having done this ritual, you will feel restored, nourished and ready to express your common-sense ideas in the most positive way.

....

APPRECIATING SENSIBILITY

♡

So how about the Virgo fear of sensibility? Common sense and 'sensibility' are very different qualities (as explored in Jane Austen's novel), and although Virgos hate to admit it, they are blessed with both, if only they would open up their feelings a little and appreciate and love their sensitive natures, too.

By acknowledging your feelings (both good and undesirable), you will be able to be of help not only to yourself, but to others, too. Here's how to appreciate and give respect and expression to all your feelings by creating a special 'me-time' niche in your home, where you can sit and enjoy feeling good about you. This is also a place to go if you feel any surges of anger or negativity; rather than ignoring or squashing them down, you can go to your niche and talk to them or express them.

You will need:
* A small mirror
* A shelf, table or just even corner of a desk
* A piece of peridot
* A piece of rose quartz
* A piece of amethyst
* A tea light

* Other votives of your choice – such as photos of family or friends, mementos, symbolic or sentimental items

1. Lean the mirror against a wall or prop it up somehow.

2. Place the three crystals in a triangle shape and put the candle in the middle.

3. Light the candle and place your chosen votives either side of the triangle.

4. Find stillness and calm and face yourself in the mirror. Appreciate who you are and what you do and be aware of your talents and skills.

5. Say the following:
I have feelings and moods like anyone else, they are not alien to me, they are part of me.
I honour my feelings and will listen to them.
If I have emotions I do not like, I will accept these are only feelings, which will come and go.
If I have emotions that I do enjoy, I will nurture them and be ready to feel them again and trust in those feelings.

6. Blow out the candle and leave your little shrine in place.

Repeat this ceremony whenever you feel that your emotions are getting on top of you. Soon, you will be appreciating your sensibility, rather than being overwhelmed by it.

. . . .

THE WELL VISUALISATION

★★
★

People know they can rely on your Virgo discretion for advice and help solving their problems. But even your busy mind can get overloaded when those around you make too many demands on your time.

The visualisation below will help to revive a little 'self-service' when you're feeling under pressure from others.

1. Imagine a deep, dark well that is constantly replenished from an underground spring.

2. Visualise yourself as this bottomless well of dedicated and genuine service to helping others. This well of you is constantly being filled from the source with compassion and a genuine desire to give of yourself. As you visualise the flowing spring water, affirm to yourself that your own love is infinite and inexhaustible. You, the well, will never run dry; and with so much to give, why not be of service to yourself, too? There is enough water in the well for everyone, including you.

3. Whenever you have a moment to yourself, use this to recall that 'self-service', or helping yourself to a little of your own well of goodness, is your right.

....

CULTIVATING SERENITY

*

For all Virgo's self-sufficient poise, you also deliver gentle kindness and an earthy mystique wherever you go. So to enhance this unique gift and attract goodness back to you, perform this little ritual, using Virgo's associated healing herbs and stones to cultivate gentleness for yourself.

You will need:
* A piece of peridot
* A lidded jar
* Fresh lemon balm leaves
* Lavender essential oil

1. Place the peridot in the jar.

2. Crumble the lemon balm leaves over the peridot.

3. Drizzle a few drops of the lavender oil over the leaves.

4. Leave overnight, and in the morning remove the stone and take it with you wherever you go.

Practise the above every new crescent moon to reinforce your enchanting demeanour. You will feel more grounded, serene and self-empowered.

Relationships

For the realistic yet sensitive Virgo, relationships are crafted and shaped by trust, utter loyalty and dedicated partnership. The cool maiden of the zodiac finds it hard to show their feelings except through the things they do for others, expecting them to prove themselves in that way, too. Self-contained Virgo needs someone who makes a lot of sense, can hold their own in a discussion or debate on anything from economics to the linguistic ability of the early primates.

Independent Virgos may be secret romantics and, often falling for the most unreliable of souls, they still believe love should be a lifelong commitment. But if the maiden of the zodiac can resist saving the mystical poet or propping up the down-at-heel artist, then their Virgo delicacy, discretion and discernment will attract the right kind of loving, loyal true partner, who can also add some fire to sensual relating. Of course, there are some Virgos who have become so independent, putting their vocation over and above their romantic longings, that they prefer single living to coupledom. But Virgos still need to be loved, no matter how self-sufficient they are.

Virgos are usually dedicated to family and friends and feel responsible for making sure everyone is happy around them. Being excellent advisors, they like to be called on to help out, but rather than looking to solve a problem (where often none exists), Virgos need to remember that sometimes pals just want a friendly chat and a big hug.

To help you attract the kind of love you are truly looking for, and care about the way you love, try the simple practices below.

....

ATTRACTING THE RIGHT
KIND OF LOVE

♡

Secret romantics or not, Virgos want to make sure they have 'found the one' before committing themselves in any way. This simple ritual means you can be sure of attracting the right kind of love to your Virgo heart, sorting out the rogues from the reliable types.

The 'claddagh ring', dating back to the seventeenth century CE, is an engagement ring or marriage band worn in Irish and Celtic folk traditions. Believed to be dropped by an eagle into the lap of a wealthy widow as a reward for her hard work (and indeed, love can be hard work for Virgos), the ring is made up of three symbols: the heart, a crown and two hands. The heart represents Virgos' need for reliability, the crown represents loyalty and the joined hands represent togetherness.

You will need:
* A piece of paper and a pen
* A rose-quartz crystal

1. On the evening of a waxing moon, place the crystal in the middle of your paper.

2. Draw a circle around the crystal.

3. On the outside of the circle, write the word 'crown' to the north of the crystal; write 'heart' to the south; and 'hand' to the east and west.

4. To show you are looking for love, draw arrows pointing outwards and inwards from each word.

5. Say the following verse as you touch the crystal with your ring finger:

With crystal's love I seek the One
Who'll come to me and share my heart.
My crown of love is filled with gold
My hands give out my heart so bold.
With all desire, send me the dove
That wings my way to be my love.

6. Take up the crystal and kiss it gently, then replace it and leave your votive in place until the full moon.

About a month later, by the next full moon, you will have attracted the right kind of person into your life for long-term love.

....

KNOW THYSELF

♡

By now, you've probably realised that your Virgo Achilles' heel is a fear of exposing your true feelings. Once you can become more aware, more honest and open about the vulnerable you behind that veil of altruism and modesty, you will find intimate relating more fulfilling.

Give yourself some wise guidance on what you want from a relationship with this self-questioning practice. Take a pen and paper and write down the following questions:

* What really matters to me in life?
* What makes me feel insecure or vulnerable?
* Which feelings am I willing to share with others?
* Which feelings do I hide from others, and from myself?
* Where do I want to be in ten years' time?
* Do I want to be alone or with a partner?
* If yes to single life, why?
* If yes to a partner, why?

Write down an honest answer beside each question. And if you don't know the answer, don't write just for the sake of it. Take time to think it over. This self-appraisal will help you to 'know' yourself. All your answers will help you to know what you truly want in love and, more importantly, why.

. . . .

SELF-CONTAINMENT

♡

Virgos fear losing track of who they are, or losing themselves in the other, so they need to feel comfortable within themselves before they can let anyone get close to them. This need to feel self-possessed is a way of saying, 'Welcome into my world, but respect my separateness'.

Here's how to safeguard your Virgo sense of completeness, so you don't lose yourself in any rush of in-loveness or in the swirling emotions of other people's energy.

You will need:
* A black candle
* A white candle
* A piece of moonstone
* A piece of black tourmaline
* Rose essential oil

1. During a waning moon, light the candles.

2. Place the moonstone in front of the black candle and the black tourmaline in front of the white candle.

3. Drizzle a few drops of the rose essential oil over the crystals.

4. Light the candles.

5. Focus and find stillness for a few minutes, as you gaze into the flames, then say:

This candle I burn to protect myself.
This candle I burn to guard inner wealth.
This candle I burn to promote good feeling.
This candle I burn to empower me with healing.
This candle I burn so I'm not lost but found.
This candle I burn for completeness all round.

6. Blow out the candles to seal your intention to the Universe and to enhance a feeling of completeness in yourself.

Follow this ritual whenever you need to maintain that sense of separateness which, ironically, means you can feel closer to someone special.

PART TWO
Caring For Your Body

...walk among long dappled grass,
And pluck till time and times are done
The silver apples of the moon
The golden apples of the sun.

W. B. Yeats, Irish poet

ere, you will discover alternative ways to look after and nurture your body, not just as a physical presence, but its connection to mind and spirit, too. This section gives you a wide range of ideas, from using sun-sign crystals to protect your physical and psychic self to fitness, diet and beauty tips. There are specific chakra practices and yoga poses especially suited to your sun sign, not forgetting bath-time rituals and calming practices to destress you and nurture holistic wellbeing.

Often obsessed with the state of their physical health (at the expense of their feelings), Virgos are very conscious of their body, beauty, shape and image and are renowned for being 'squeaky clean'. Virgo rules the intestines, bowels, solar plexus and diaphragm, so it's understandable that the old adage 'you are what you eat' is probably mostly relevant to Virgos. And their acute sensitivity to any twinge or ache in their body means if a Virgo's health is not in tip-top condition, anxiety will set in.

When Virgos pay attention to their holistic health, they find fewer chinks in their polished armour. Working out and getting fit can help to express all that nervous energy, so if there's no local gym to turn to, your own weights and indoor bike at home are, for you, the way to go. Pampering and loving your body beautiful will also mean you can show off to others your knowledge of every new body-care product under the sun.

Fitness and Movement

A daily morning ritual helps Virgos feel in control of their lives, and structured fitness workouts suit their need for routine and more routine. If you feel you don't have time to do a complete yoga, Pilates or simple warm-up stretching session every day (usually thirty minutes is recommended), target upper arms and shoulder stretches one day, core the next and so on. You may like to fit in twice-weekly (or more) sessions at the gym (exercise bikes, muscle flexers, weights and all) or indulge in a focused sport such as tennis or badminton to clear your mind of worrying thoughts. You can also benefit from gardening or a blissful walk in the country to help calm the mind and balance energy levels.

Having said all this, don't beat yourself up about missing a day; it's not going to be life-changing!

Here are some simple practices to nurture your holistic fitness.

....

SINGING AND DANCING IN THE RAIN

★★
★

Virgos are thought to have beautiful singing voices, due to their association with the god Hermes. (The god of eloquence sang and played his lyre so beautifully that Apollo exchanged his stolen cattle for ownership of the musical instrument.) Exercising your vocal cords will release tension from your neck and shoulder muscles, while free-form dancing will liberate your senses and strengthen all aspects of your physique.

You may already have an idea of a song that has meaning to you, have a melody in your head you just want to 'la la la' to or have a whole opera to perform, but whatever it is, you will feel the release of all that nervous energy into the landscape.

1. On a rainy day, dress however you like, go outside and find a place where you feel you can sing without anyone bothering you. (Choose somewhere you won't feel embarrassed, observed or judged by anyone.)

2. Stand or walk in the rain and begin to sing your chosen song or just improvise.

3. Once you have warmed up your voice, start to dance. This can be any style you like, free form, a twist, ballet – whatever brings you delight.

As you sing and dance, you will feel vitalised – and not only will you exercise your voice, but the rain will stimulate your skin, and you will feel 'in tune' with yourself overall.

....

A NORDIC WALK

★★
★★

One of the greatest, easiest and most beneficial of Virgo practices for physical self-care is walking in the great outdoors.

Nordic walking employs ski-like poles to propel you along with grace and poise. It is also a way to combine cardiovascular exercise with a vigorous muscle workout for your shoulders, arms, core and legs. Whereas normal walking activates the muscles below the waist, with Nordic poles you activate all your upper-body muscles for overall toning. It is also a gentle form of aerobic exercise that can be done anywhere and at any time.

This practice includes a few extra exercises to amplify the beneficial effects of Nordic walking.

1. Before you start your walk, stand straight and raise both the poles horizontally above the top of your head with both hands (as if you're lifting weights), then return them to head height. Do this in time to a rhythmic out-breath when up and down to the in-breath. Repeat 20 times.

2. Next, hold the poles above your head and then bring them down horizontally in front of your body and back up above your head again. Repeat 20 times.

3. Finally, hold the poles above your head and lower them down behind your head, as far as your arms will stretch down. Repeat 20 times.

Now you have toned up your arm, neck and back muscles, ready for your great walk!

....

YOGA: FOLDING OVER

★★
★

This pose not only stimulates and tones those Virgo digestive organs, but also relaxes the busy mind and calms any nervous anxiety.

1. Sit on the floor with your legs straight out in front of you, feet flexed with toes towards you and your sit bones on the floor, so your spine is straight.

2. Inhale and slowly bend forwards from the hips.

3. If you can, grab your toes and pull yourself down and forwards; if you can't quite stretch to the toes, grab the sides of your feet or your shins.

4. With each inhale, lengthen your torso and fold over further, so your torso gets closer to your knees and your head closer to your shins. Hold this pose for about two minutes, and then gradually unwind.

5. Return to sitting, then to a cross-legged seat before you stand up.

After practising this pose, you will feel supple, stretched and composed.

Nutrition

Rigorous about high standards of food and hygiene, Virgos research all the latest diet and nutritional fads and ensure they have immaculate kitchens to match. Their kitchen cupboards are often filled with as many alternative supplements as they are with food, simply because although they eat well, they are always worried they aren't getting enough of this or that mineral or vitamin. Busy Virgos have a habit of popping down to the local health-food shop, fine delicatessen or sushi bar to buy the best produce available and catch up on the latest gossip – a good way to feed their inquisitive and acquisitive minds, too. Seeing that Virgos are well aware of the value they place on nutrition for good health, their goals are centred around not fussing about what they eat, and making a conscious effort to not control their eating habits to such an extent that it interferes with their enjoyment of life. A few guilty pleasures now and then will do a Virgo a world of good.

....

LIST IT

✳

Virgo is a controlling sign, and eating can sometimes be used as a way to feel in control of life to compensate for any sense of disorder or mess elsewhere. To avoid this pitfall, listen to your body's needs. If you want to control something, then make lists of what foods are good for you; make a rota of what you can eat and when, and maybe even a list of dos and don'ts on your fridge. It's fine to control the ingredients you use and plan around your eating habits, but don't fall foul of an actual obsession with eating habits.

....

MAGIC WATER BOTTLE

✳

Every well-informed Virgo knows the important of hydrating the body, and usually carries a water bottle of some description with them wherever they go. You may have dispensed with the plastic kind already, but whatever you take on your travels, try this simple ritual to inspirit your water with health-giving Earth energy before you set off.

You will need:
* A reusable cup, flask or bottle with lid
* A piece of clear quartz crystal (removes geopathic stress)
* A piece of smoky quartz (for vitalising Earth energy)
* A piece of aquamarine (for clarity and purity)

1. Prepare your bottle as normal (wash and dry off).

2. With your crystals, create a triangle pattern (large enough to surround the diameter of the cup or flask), placing the clear quartz to the north, the smoky quartz to the south-east and the aquamarine to the south-west.

85

3. Place the flask or bottle in the centre and say, 'With every sip of this water my body is hydrated, cleansed and purified by the power of the crystal energy'.

4. Remove the flask or bottle from the crystal grid.

Your flask is now imbued with crystal power. Before you sip the water, say the affirmation in step 3 again; you will feel washed clean of all toxins and drink in the true joy of purified living.

Beauty

Even if they appear modest about their image, make-up and dress sense in a cool, elegant and classic way, most Virgos have bathrooms filled with organic or natural beauty products. In fact, you probably know more about the benefits of skin and nail care than most other signs of the zodiac. And you also know that beauty begins within: nourishing your body isn't just about slapping on an avocado face mask (although it is that, too), but pampering and nurturing all aspects of you.

Here are some inspiring ways to enhance, cherish, care for and bring out the best of your elegant Virgo self.

....

BEAUTY SLEEP

♡

A good night's sleep is one of the best beauty makeovers a Virgo can get, as it removes all those daily worries and restores equilibrium. The following tips will ensure you get the best possible dream and sleep time.

1. Make sure your bedroom is free of clutter. Virgo is such a sensitive sign, and when disorder reigns in the home, the mere thought of it can disrupt their sleep. So even if you're one of those Virgos who lives in 'organised chaos', declutter and tidy up, so you can sleep peacefully without worrying about the mess.

2. Just before bedtime, run a warm, nurturing bath with your favourite products, adding an essential oil blend of rose hip, frankincense and lavender to enhance soft skin; treat yourself to a little ritualistic glass of something you fancy; and put on your favourite relaxing music.

3. Drizzle a couple of drops of lavender oil on to your sheets, and one under your pillow for its calming, soothing sleep properties.

4. Always make sure you don't sleep under a large supporting beam or joist (they carry negative energy) or have a mirror facing the end of the bed (this bounces energy around the room and will prevent restful sleep).

Follow the above, and you can rest assured that your sleep time will be beneficial to all aspects of the beautiful you.

....

A TOUCH OF PERIDOT

♡

Meticulous Virgos need a careful, precise skincare regime. To give your skin the attention it deserves, add the healing power of the crystal, peridot, to your routine. Jade and other crystal rollers have become essential accessories for us all, but here you will use your own zodiac-sign stone to imbue you with elegance.

You will need:
* 5 tablespoons of sweet almond oil
* 4 drops of sandalwood essential oil
* A lidded jar
* A small piece of peridot

1. Mix the oils in the jar.

2. Place the peridot in the jar and leave overnight to imbue the crystal with the oils' rejuvenating powers.

3. The next day, take out the peridot and cleanse and tone your face with the crystal: use gentle circling movements with the most blunt, rounded or flat part of the stone.

Your face will be cleansed and nourished with both the oils' skin-softening benefits and the stone's calming energy. You will feel revitalised and exude a true Virgo crystal glow.

CHAKRA BALANCE

The body's chakras are the epicentres of the life-force energy that flows through all things (see p. 22).

Virgo is mostly associated with the throat chakra of communication. This chakra is concerned with the way we put our messages across, our interaction with the world and how objective or subjective we are.

When this chakra is underactive, you may find it hard to understand other people's problems and may – unusually – not offer to help; shyness may overcome you and you may prefer your own company, avoiding social events. To reinforce and balance this chakra, carry or wear red carnelian (symbolising passion) to promote confidence and your genuine desire to care for the underdog.

If you have an overactive throat chakra, you may find people's mistakes intolerable, question their beliefs, be overly critical or not let anyone else have their say. To subdue this energy, restore harmonious relating and enhance greater understanding of others, carry or wear blue lace agate (for acceptance).

Balancing this chakra will not only boost Virgo physical and mental health, but also bring you better relationships.

General Wellbeing

For the hard-working and body-conscious Virgo, priding yourself on your neat, classic appearance gives you a sense of wellbeing, as do the decor and organisation of your home. Caring for your home as a sanctuary will bring harmony to all aspects of your life, protecting you from environmental pollution (geopathic stress and negativity from other people), while also creating positive energy around you. Here are two practices to promote a more serene, relaxed you.

. . . .

ENHANCE GOOD VIBES

★★
★

Traditionally, candles, oils and resins have been burned to arouse feelings of love, calm, desire and happiness. This incense and crystal grid (a symbolic pattern that amplifies the energy of the crystals and their properties required) will balance your Virgo qualities of warmth and contentment and set a harmonious atmosphere for the home.

You will need:
* 6 pieces of rose-quartz crystal (for warmth and closeness)
* 6 pieces of moss agate (for harmony)
* 2 drops of ylang yang essential oil (for love)
* 2 drops of sandalwood essential oil (to calm the mind)

1. With five of each of the different stones, form two circles – one inside the other (it doesn't matter which you choose as the outer or inner ring).

2. Place the sixth stone of each type in the centre.

3. Drop the ylang ylang and sandalwood oil on to the central crystals.

4. Relax in the room for a while, taking in the scent and indulging in the calming ambience.

Leave the grid in place for as long as you like and, if you ever need to relax and centre yourself, your home and family, repeat the ritual as above. Ensuring that the holistic health of mind, body and spirit is safeguarded, this home enhancement will bring your feelings and moods into harmony, too, invoking Virgo wellbeing via the senses.

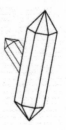

....

THE FILING CABINET VISUALISATION

★⋆
⋆

Even a discerning, polished Virgo gets sidetracked from their mindful goals by taking time out (and so you should), socialising, enjoying the company of others and, of course, dating. But if you ever get that feeling of being disconnected from your priorities, or that life's getting a bit chaotic because you need to sort out your work–life balance before it all overwhelms you, use this visualisation to get your mind back on track.

1. Sit somewhere quiet, and imagine you are standing in front of a large filing cabinet. Inside the cabinet are all your thoughts, ideas, feelings, worries, priorities, needs and so on, all carefully filed away. You know that as soon as you pull open the drawer you can put your finger on what you are looking for without even 'thinking' about it.

2. Now imagine yourself opening a drawer – the one you instinctively know will put your thoughts back into order.

3. See the drawer open, see yourself take out a file and open it; see how clearly your goals and plans for the future are laid out before you. In your imagination, you will see how to map out the day or the week ahead, or how to prioritise family, work, life or fun.

Now come out of the visualisation and you will feel destressed, relaxed and ready to get your life back on track.

PART THREE

Caring For Your Soul

There is something at work in my soul, which I do not understand.

Mary Shelley, English novelist

This final section offers you tailored, fun, easy and amazing ways to connect to and care for your sacred self. This, in turn, means you will begin to feel at one with the joyous energy of the Universe. You don't have to sign up to any religion or belief system (unless you want to) – just take some time to experience uplifting moments through your interaction with the spiritual aspects of the cosmos. Care for your sun sign's soul centre, and you care about the Universe, too.

There is a sceptical side to Virgo that says, 'How can I categorise and label something which is numinous? Or even begin to predict the future by gazing into a crystal ball?' But actually, secretly you're drawn to all things supernatural, spiritual and magical, simply because – believe it or not – a dreamy, sensitive soul lies beneath that cool, unruffled, intellectual approach to life.

Studying astrology or even divining patterns in Nature may confirm to you that the cosmos is, in fact, orderly and that maybe some divine being, or Mother Nature, is pretty tidy, too. Caring for what might be, as well as what is and what was, will unify all the bits of you that you so long to piece together into one big Virgo finished jigsaw puzzle. So do yourself a huge favour and open up to the possibility of soul – for in the deepest part of yourself, you know you have something divine flowing through you. In fact, the Virgo facade conceals a latent inner mystic, and now is the time to embrace her.

Here are some practices to get in touch with your sacred self and use the magic of the mysteries of life in the so-called 'real world'. These will also help you to accept and nurture the sacred you, where your potential for fulfilment can be truly found.

A FORAGING PRACTICE

✳

Foraging isn't just about harvesting, finding seeds or cuttings to grow; as long as you take care not to harvest rare or protected species or pick poisonous plants or fungi, it will enable you to forge a stronger bond with Nature and the divine that flows through everything.

Foraging is a gift given by the Universe, enabling us to see the Earth as a reflection of ourselves, whether in cultivated gardens (our culture, beliefs, logic and ability to relate to others) or wilder places (our feelings, our spirits, souls and mystery). So respect, give gratitude and love the gifts you find in the wilder places because the wild, weedy, stony places are part of you, too.

Rummaging around in Nature is a very simple but special way of finding the Virgo sacred self.

1. Go out into the countryside, a park, garden or green space and collect a few stones. They don't have to be anything special – just stones that you come across. Maybe they 'say' something to you, you feel as if you are 'meant' to pick them up or they stand out from the surrounding terrain or other stones in some way. Maybe, in fact, the stones are choosing you, as much as you are choosing them.

2. When you get home, wash and dry your precious foraged stones. Place them in a circle or a small pile in a dedicated space. You don't have to 'use' them for anything other than to meditate or reflect upon. They are reminders of your connection to Nature and the divine that permeates all things.

3. As you reflect, say, 'With these wild stones, I can now begin to see the mystery within myself and honour and connect to this place'.

Leave your little shrine to spiritual mystery in place, and as you pass it by every day, you will feel more and more enriched in spirit and soul.

....

THE GODDESS IN YOU

♡

If Virgo has long been linked to fertility and Earth goddesses such as Demeter, the sign is also embodied in the so-called 'triple goddess' symbol of maiden, mother and crone, associated with three of the phases of the moon. The triple goddess also 'fits' the Virgo cycle of 'creating' (the maiden), 'producing' (the mother) and 'making use of that wisdom' (the crone). So use the triple goddess archetype to discover a new connection to your sacred self and to promote greater creativity.

You will need:
* A piece of paper and a pen
* A symbol of the triple goddess (you can find one online)
* 3 green tea lights
* 3 pieces of peridot

1. On the evening of a waxing moon, draw a large version of the triple goddess symbol.

2. Place the lit candles and a piece of peridot on each of the three moon phases.

3. Reflect on your creative ideas to invoke a sense of inner union of mind, body, spirit and soul.

4. Now focus on each of the three crystals in turn. As you gaze at the first, say: 'My intention is to create'; as you gaze at the second, say: 'My intention is to produce'; as you gaze at the third, say: 'My intention is to make use of my wisdom'.

5. When you have reflected on your intention for a minute or so, blow out the candles.

After practising this ritual, you will feel at one with an inner place of self-reliance, containment and self-belief. It can be performed at any time of the lunar cycle to restore the spirit of creativity.

....

A SPIRITUAL PATHWAY

In the physical world, Virgos prefer well-lit pathways to dark alleys. Similarly, in the spiritual realm, your mercurial mind might benefit from a clear pathway, too. The interconnecting spheres of the mystical Kabbalah (made up of thirty-two pathways) are said to represent a route to spiritual illumination. There are ten 'doorways' linking these pathways, known as the 'sephiroth', which are used as symbolic entry points on this spiritual journey.

The following ritual replicates the symbolic pattern of the sephiroth and will help you to experience new dimensions of your spiritual journey.

You will need:
* 10 white tea lights
* 10 clear quartz crystals

1. Position the candles to form the common symbolic pattern of the Kabbalah (you can find this online).

2. Light the candles and, as you do so, focus on each one in turn, saying, each time you light one, 'This light brings me spiritual healing and balance'.

3. Place a crystal in front of each tea light.

4. Meditate or focus on the crystals and the candles for a few minutes.

5. Once you have relaxed and focused, blow the candles out, one by one. As you do so, you will feel the light of the universal healing energy enter your world.

Perform this ritual during a waxing-moon phase to enhance spiritual empowerment and healing.

Last Words

Self-care for Virgo is, of course, about promoting your good work, tending to others' needs and creating some order in the chaos of life – but don't forget to love yourself first. Because with self-love and understanding, you will also be giving out genuine care, and this will give you a sense of wholeness and wellbeing.

This book has shown you that yes, you do care about your physical wellbeing, you do care about how you look and the impression you make on the world, but are you really acknowledging and caring for the vulnerable, emotional you inside? Like the famous Virgo, Queen Elizabeth I, who likened herself to 'a rock that bends to no wind', you too have this innate strength to remain poised and unmovable in the face of any dilemma. You may already be a bit of a 'rock' in your relationships and working life, but are you as solid and as confident in your emotional one?

This book has shown you that facing your feelings and expressing them will bring you more than poise;

it will free you from self-doubt and self-reproach and generate love for your true Virgo autonomy.

Most of all, Virgo is a sign of profound, earthy mysticism and, once in touch with that spiritual or sacred place within, you will discover how uplifted and enlightened it will make you feel. Connecting to your sacred self will empower you with the happiness you seek.

If you care truly for who you are first, and everyone else second, your integrity and authenticity will flourish, and you will enjoy becoming who you are: a child of the autumn – an embodiment of the 'season of mists and mellow fruitfulness'. Time to reap the beautiful benefits of your own harvest.

Resources

Main sites for crystals, stones, candles, smudging sticks, incense, pouches, essential oils and everything needed for the holistic self-care practices included this book:

holisticshop.co.uk
thepsychictree.co.uk
thesoulangels.co.uk
earthcrystals.com
livrocks.com
artisanaromatics.com

For a substantial range of books (and metaphysical items) on astrology, divination, runes, palmistry, tarot and holistic health, etc.:

thelondonastrologyshop.com
watkinsbooks.com
mysteries.co.uk
barnesandnoble.com
innertraditions.com

For more information on astrology, personal horo-
scopes and birth-chart calculations:
astro-charts.com (simplest, very user friendly)

horoscopes.astro-seek.com
(straightforward)
astrolibrary.org/free-birth-chart
(easy to use, with lots of extra information)

Glossary

Aura An invisible electromagnetic energy field that emanates from and surrounds all living beings

Auric power The dominant colour of the aura that reveals your current mood or state

Chakra Sanskrit for 'wheel', in Eastern spiritual traditions the seven chakras are the main epicentres – or wheels – of invisible energy throughout the body

Dark of the moon This is when the moon is invisible to us, due to its proximity to the sun; it is a time for reflection, solitude and a deeper awareness of oneself

Divination Gaining insight into the past, present and future using symbolic or esoteric means

Double-terminator crystal A quartz crystal with a point at each end, allowing its energy to flow both ways

Full moon The sun is at its maximum opposition to the moon, thus casting light across all of the moon's orb; in esoteric terms, it is a time for culmination, finalising deals, committing to love and so on

Geopathic stress Negative energy emanating from and on the Earth, such as underground water courses, tunnels, overhead electrical cables and geological faults

Grid A specific pattern or layout of items symbolising specific intentions or desires

Horoscope An astrological chart or diagram showing the position of the sun, moon and planets at the time of any given event, such as the moment of somebody's birth, a marriage or the creation of an enterprise; it is used to interpret the characteristics or to forecast the future of that person or event

New crescent moon A fine sliver of crescent light that appears curving outwards to the right in the northern hemisphere and to the left in the southern hemisphere; this phase is for beginning new projects, new romance, ideas and so on

Psychic energy One's intuition, sixth sense or instincts, as well as the divine, numinous or magical power that flows through everything

Shadow side In astrology, your shadow side describes those aspects of your personality associated with your opposite sign and of which you are not usually aware

Smudging Clearing negative energy from the home with a smouldering bunch of dried herbs, such as sage

Solar return salutation A way to give thanks and welcome the sun's return to your zodiac sign once a year (your birthday month)

Sun in opposition The sun as it moves through the opposite sign to your own sun sign

Sun sign The zodiac sign through which the sun was moving at the exact moment of your birth

Waning moon The phase of the moon after it is full, when it begins to lose its luminosity – the waning moon is illuminated on its left side in the northern hemisphere, and on its right side in the southern hemisphere; this is a time for letting go, acceptance and preparing to start again

Waxing moon The phase between a new and a full moon, when it grows in luminosity – the waxing moon is illuminated on its right side in the northern hemisphere and on its left side in the southern hemisphere; this is a time for putting ideas and desires into practice

Zodiac The band of sky divided into twelve segments (known as the astrological signs), along which the paths of the sun, the moon and the planets appear to move

About the Author

After studying at the Faculty of Astrological Studies in London, the UK, Sarah gained the Diploma in Psychological Astrology – an in-depth 3-year professional training programme cross-fertilised by the fields of astrology and depth, humanistic and transpersonal psychology. She has worked extensively in the media as astrologer for titles such as *Cosmopolitan* magazine (UK), *SHE, Spirit & Destiny* and the *London Evening Standard*, and appeared on UK TV and radio shows, including *Steve Wright in the Afternoon* on BBC Radio 2.

Her mainstream mind-body-spirit books include the international bestsellers, *The Tarot Bible, The Little Book of Practical Magic* and *Secrets of the Universe in 100 Symbols*.

Sarah currently practises and teaches astrology and other esoteric arts in the heart of the countryside.

Acknowledgements

I would first like to thank everyone at Yellow Kite, Hodder & Stoughton and Hachette UK who were part of the process of creating this series of twelve zodiac self-care books. I am especially grateful to Carolyn Thorne for the opportunity to write these guides; Anne Newman for her editorial advice, which kept me 'carefully' on the right track; and Olivia Nightingall who kept me on target for everything else! It is when people come together with their different skills and talents that the best books are made – so I am truly grateful for being part of this team.